A
WALK
IN THE
DARK

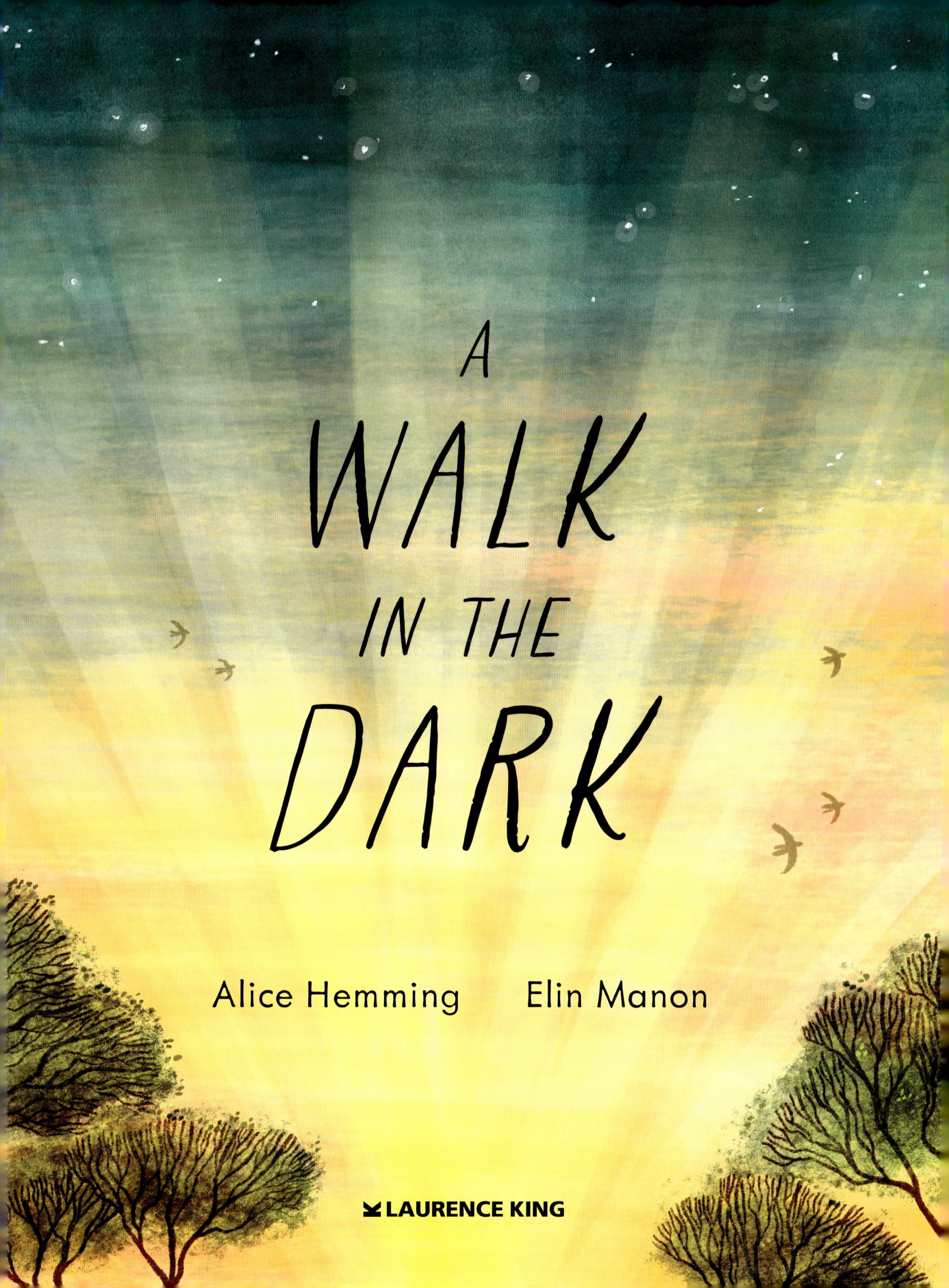

A WALK IN THE DARK

Alice Hemming Elin Manon

LAURENCE KING

It's *TWILIGHT* – the day is nearly done. As the sun sinks below the horizon, a soft warm glow fills the sky.

Life slows down
in the human world.
Families gather around
tables. Lights appear in
windows and curtains close.

But these rabbits are just
beginning to come out.

They have spent most of their day UNDERGROUND . . .

Rabbits are **crepuscular,** which means they are most active at dawn and dusk.

and now they are ready to hop, play and nibble grass.

One rabbit spots a *FOX!*

A loud THUMP from the rabbit's foot warns the rest of the group.

In a flash, they scatter,
white tails bobbing as they
disappear into burrows.

Underground, the rabbits
are sheltered and safe from
predators. Rabbit burrows
are cool in the summer and
warm in the winter.

The fox will have to look elsewhere for her meal.

*Foxes are **omnivores:** they eat everything, including worms, insects, fruit and berries.*

But she is a *SCAVENGER* as well as a hunter and it doesn't take her long! She finds some chicken remains that people have thrown away.

The *VIXEN* (female fox) brings the meal home to her cubs. The foxes' underground den was once part of a badger's *SETT*. In fact, badgers still live there!

Badgers build large setts with complicated tunnels and chambers that can take years to complete. They even dig a special **'latrine'** hole for their dung.

It's fully dark now. A badger sniffs his way along this well-trodden scent path to search for worms in the open field.

He doesn't spot the mouse.
She *JUMPS* quickly away.

*Wood mice can stand on their
back legs to check for danger and
sometimes jump distances of up to
80 cm (31 inches) to avoid predators.*

The mouse is small and there are many predators out at night. Not all of them are on the ground. She darts into the hedgerow to avoid this barn owl, which is gliding soundlessly over the field.

Barn owls don't 'toowhitt' or
'toowhoo' like tawny owls, but they
do make all sorts of other noises like
screeching, whistling and snoring!

The owl quickly finds another meal.
Although she can see well in the dark,
she uses sound to detect her prey.

So do these pipistrelle bats. They use *ECHOLOCATION* to sense the world around them, which is why they make very high-pitched noises, usually too high for humans to hear.

These noises 'hit' objects and bounce back like an ECHO.

Bats are the only true flying mammals. Flying squirrels and flying lemurs actually glide rather than fly.

The bat is looking for insects.

She will eat about 3,000 insects tonight but she'll avoid these beautiful fireflies – they would make her sick.

*In Europe, fireflies are often known as **glow-worms**. But a firefly isn't a fly or a worm. It's a beetle.*

It's very dark here, with no artificial
lights and just a sliver of moon.
Ideal conditions for the fireflies.
They glow to attract mates but also
to show that they don't taste very nice!

They aren't the only insects out at night. This MOTH is looking for flowers.

There are around
160,000 species
of moth! Most of them
are nocturnal.

The moth drinks nectar from the flowers
with its long tongue. It is a *POLLINATOR*,
doing a similar job to butterflies.

*Moths are drawn to
light-coloured flowers that
reflect any moonlight.*

It carries pollen from
flower to flower as it feeds,
helping the flowers reproduce.

Nearby, a spider has built her web near this night light in the hope of catching insects like the moth that are drawn to the light.

This spider is a
garden orb-weaver.
*Their webs can be large —
up to 40 cm (15 inches) in
diameter.*

The spider feels the
vibrations from her web.
Is this her next meal?

No — it was a cat! The spider has some work to do to rebuild her web. It may take her a couple of hours. But the cat has moved on.

Cats have excellent vision in low light levels as well as good balance, flexibility and speed. This allows them to take some surprising shortcuts!

The cat is getting hungry.
He yowls at the window until
his tired human lets him in.

Humans are **diurnal**. We are active
during the day and like to sleep at night
when we can! The opposite of diurnal
is **nocturnal,** which is being active at
night and sleeping during the day.

It's *DAWN* – a new day is beginning.
As the sun peeps over the horizon,
birds are singing their dawn chorus
and some animals are just waking up,
after a good night's rest.

PROTECTING OUR NIGHT SKIES

Pollution is caused when harmful substances are released into the environment. We often hear about water, land and air pollution and we do what we can to help protect our seas and the air around us. But have you ever heard of light pollution?

Light pollution is where artificial light from buildings, cars and streetlights shines into our night skies. This stops us from being able to see the stars above and can affect our sleeping patterns. It also wastes energy and is very confusing for wildlife. Light pollution is a problem all over the world and is worst in towns and cities.

The good news is that there is a lot that can be done to stop this type of pollution. Experts are working hard to protect the skies above.

There are things you can do to help:

- Find out about the sky at night. It is fascinating!
- Encourage adults to use warm, not cool light, and to point lights only where they are needed (not into the night sky).
- Switch off lights when you're not using them or use timers and sensors where possible.
- Look after nocturnal animals by pointing lights away from green spaces.

Turn the page to find more ways you can help nocturnal animals.

HOW YOU CAN HELP NOCTURNAL ANIMALS

Many of the animals in this book are nocturnal, which means they are active at night and sleep during the day. Nocturnal animals face a lot of the same threats as diurnal animals, like destruction of their habitats (homes), but they also face other problems caused by light pollution. For example:

- Some prey animals rely on darkness to protect them from predators.
- Animals that migrate, like birds and turtles, need to use moonlight or starlight to find their way. When they can't see the stars, they get confused.
- Many insects are drawn to artificial light and can die of exhaustion, circling the lights. This in turn has an effect on other animals and plants in the food chain which would eat these insects or rely on them for pollination.

You can help nocturnal animals in many ways:
- Do what you can to prevent light pollution (see previous page).
- If you have any outside space, let a little area grow wild to provide hiding places.
- Provide water for nocturnal animals to drink and bathe.
- Grow plants, which look lovely and attract insects.

PROTECTING OUR NIGHT SKIES

Pollution is caused when harmful substances are released into the environment. We often hear about water, land and air pollution and we do what we can to help protect our seas and the air around us. But have you ever heard of light pollution?

Light pollution is where artificial light from buildings, cars and streetlights shines into our night skies. This stops us from being able to see the stars above and can affect our sleeping patterns. It also wastes energy and is very confusing for wildlife. Light pollution is a problem all over the world and is worst in towns and cities.

The good news is that there is a lot that can be done to stop this type of pollution. Experts are working hard to protect the skies above.

There are things you can do to help:

- Find out about the sky at night. It is fascinating!
- Encourage adults to use warm, not cool light, and to point lights only where they are needed (not into the night sky).
- Switch off lights when you're not using them or use timers and sensors where possible.
- Look after nocturnal animals by pointing lights away from green spaces.

Turn the page to find more ways you can help nocturnal animals.

HOW YOU CAN HELP NOCTURNAL ANIMALS

Many of the animals in this book are nocturnal, which means they are active at night and sleep during the day. Nocturnal animals face a lot of the same threats as diurnal animals, like destruction of their habitats (homes), but they also face other problems caused by light pollution. For example:

- Some prey animals rely on darkness to protect them from predators.
- Animals that migrate, like birds and turtles, need to use moonlight or starlight to find their way. When they can't see the stars, they get confused.
- Many insects are drawn to artificial light and can die of exhaustion, circling the lights. This in turn has an effect on other animals and plants in the food chain which would eat these insects or rely on them for pollination.

You can help nocturnal animals in many ways:
- Do what you can to prevent light pollution (see previous page).
- If you have any outside space, let a little area grow wild to provide hiding places.
- Provide water for nocturnal animals to drink and bathe.
- Grow plants, which look lovely and attract insects.

For Simon, with love.

A.H.

LAURENCE KING

First published in Great Britain and the US in 2025 by Laurence King

Text copyright © Alice Hemming 2025
Illustration copyright © Elin Manon 2025

Alice Hemming and Elin Manon have asserted their rights
under the Copyright, Designs and Patents Act 1988,
to be identified as the author and illustrator of this work.

HB ISBN: 978-1-510-23148-1
Ebook ISBN: 978-1-510-23149-8

10 9 8 7 6 5 4 3 2 1

Printed in China

FSC
www.fsc.org

MIX
Paper | Supporting
responsible forestry
FSC® C104740

Laurence King
An imprint of Hachette Children's Group
Part of Hodder and Stoughton Limited
Carmelite House
50 Victoria Embankment
London EC4Y 0DZ

An Hachette UK Company
www.hachette.co.uk
www.hachettechildrens.co.uk
www.laurenceking.com

The authorised representative in the EEA is Hachette Ireland,
8 Castlecourt Centre, Dublin 15, D15 XTP3, Ireland
(email: info@hbgi.ie)